CUPID, GROWN

Adam Panichi is a British poet and social worker based between the UK and Italy. A runner-up in the Ledbury and Brotherton poetry prizes, his work has been widely published in poetry journals including *And Other Poems*, *berlin lit*, *Strix*, *fourteen poems*, and *Magma*. *Cupid, Grown*, which was shortlisted in the Poetry London Pamphlet Prize, is Adam's debut.

ISBN: 978-1-917617-01-7

Cover designed by Aaron Kent

Cover image: © Rrose Selavy / Adobe Stock

Edited and Typeset by Aaron Kent

Broken Sleep Books Ltd
PO BOX 102
Llandysul
SA44 9BG

CONTENTS

for Riccardo

"And after he had laid his hand on mine,
with joyful mien, whence I was comforted,
he led me in among the secret things."
— Dante, Inferno

Cupid, Grown

Adam Panichi

Broken Sleep Books

CUPID, GROWN

In youth my leaf was smooth as a Ken doll's. I was Cupid then,
saw myself through a hand mirror. No one can other you
quite like yourself. In the hot keen night, I would fold the thing
between my legs into the neck of a swan asleep. The god of love emasc-
ulated; I tried to give myself to men. Men at my father's football club,
potent with Deep Heat's musk, swung fat cocks around the showers,
soaping them the way a warrior whets his blade.
Romans wore amulets of the phallic divine, dangled tintinnabula
in doorways, from horses when they rode in battle. I too have offered
a pinch of flour, hung one around my own neck, hoping.
But now I'm Eros, virile, god of desire—
playful in the mirror. I've untucked myself. Watch me
rattle my train of blisteringly coloured feathers.
I drink whiskey. I shave my chest. I put men on their knees.

i. Cupid

THE BOYS ARE KILLING THEIR SIMS ON THE FAMILY PC
after Andrew McMillan

Legs crossed under their computer desks
like a pole dancer in an ankle hang, sweating
as if the floor has been deleted,
running their hands over their silken midriff
in the character room's mirror, deciding between
the kitten heel and the thigh high boot. *It's okay.*
Out of view the door is locked, the boys
are taking up floristry, selling their creations,
their prickled thumbs, gardens fragrant
with box shrubs and lavender.
There's no gravestone under the oak tree
so there's no ghost to haunt the lot at night.
They've just finished renovating the guest bathroom
— *aren't the tiles to die for?* — have found
the perfect fuchsia paper for the hall.
How gorgeous their home is when no one's in.
The boys are flirting with Don Lothario, *shh*
Nina has no idea! They've bought a heart-shaped bed,
invited their lovers over. The boys cannot wait
to raise a child, are petrified to the point
of stillness, they've moved the cot beside their bed,
the media terrified the boys will mimic
what they do behind their screens.
No longer wary of fireplaces or pools of water,
when they talk about Bella Goth, the boys
are mixing up their pronouns. If the new sofa
doesn't go, they can always pick a new one.
I feel for all our drowning.

DEAD DOGS

My childhood home is full
of dead dogs.

Mum keeps hers in an urn
on the sideboard, says
one day she'll scatter him—
he's still there in the dining room
waiting.

Dead dogs would hang
from dad's chandelier,
if he had chandeliers.

(Instead, they hang from lampshades)

When I go back and take a bath,
dead Labradors climb the plug hole.
I try not to wash when I visit.

(I stink of dead dog)

Don't you dare dig up
the garden plants, I can't face
their empty graves.

I will never let a dog
within fifty feet of my home.

(I trawl through shelters)

My parents collected so many dead dogs,
they were forced to buy
separate houses, new duvets
to hide their dead dogs.

(Air so thick family meals are gritty)

I fear ashes are like spores:
a dead dog is growing.

LILAC BUSHES

I've got a lot of making up to do
— William Leslie Arnold

Behind the vinyl shower curtain a lilac bush,
knotted into the tie around your neck a lilac bush,

floating in the cereal a lilac bush, on the cheek you kiss
your son on before work and halfway

through your favourite jazz record where it skips
a lilac bush. At the school recital you've never missed,

at parent-teacher conference, blossoming from the teacher's
mouth a lilac bush. When you make love to your wife

her skin is lilac fragranced, isn't it? Playing ball with your son
on the lawn, the lawn a lilac meadow. In the kitchen

your wife makes dinner, you wonder how she does it
all those lilac bushes on the counter. During

a sermon on the sinfulness of crime, a lilac bush at the pulpit.
When you pass an airport, cop car or penitentiary.

On every remembered anniversary.
As the reed touches your lips to play, lilac's taste.

William, when the detective finally found
you, someone had laid flowers on your grave.

COTTON-COLLARED MAFIOSI

It only mattered
that it'd been drawn by a kid
lesser than me.

A ginger boy
not a probable fag.
There's a pecking order—

all ten-year-olds know this,
every classroom a crime den,
kids cotton-collared mafiosi.

Jake had written
'Adam is a faggot'
in the bike shed's morning breath

childish finger an ice pick.
Mrs Elison found me
bleeding under my sweater

made me list names
like an FBI informant,
every boy who'd ever cut me.

I left his off.

Then I went
to the stationery drawer, took out
the Staedtler.

BIBBIDI-BOBBIDI-BOO

Float down the steps
cabin bed queen
Dad's old slogan tee swishing
at your scabby knees

You've never looked so
honest, it's serving waist

Mum's tasseled tieback,
scrunched football sock shelf

Don't prick ears like woodland prey
to the landing floor, catch
yourself in the mirrored door

> *I'll always love you*
> *just the same, but...*

Watch, the room spangles

rags fizzle
ivory sissying clean
hemline to neck, see it lace

elbow, prepubescent
wrist

> *...you're not one of the camp*
> *ones, are you?*

Hush, it isn't yet midnight—

touch glass
as if they could pass through it

THE FIRST EMPRESS OF ROME THROWS A GENDER REVEAL

Call me not Lord, for I am a Lady.
— Elagabalus

Too young for such declarations,
whose own tongue is not to be believed—

in whose chamber cosmetae
rouged the apples of the young ruler's
cheeks, who batted kohl black lashes

cruel as any man or woman could be

who, on seeing their face shaved bare,
held a decadent feast

where guests drank wine and were buried so deep
in falling blossoms that some were smothered, dead

who, abandoned
to the grossest pleasures, bed
goddesses and men—

trapped in bronze, a strange boy's bust on every coin,
offering half the empire to the physician
able to re-form the clay
between her legs:

Elagabalus, whose brutalised body
sank beneath the uncaring Tiber.

BATHHOUSE

Steam rises, a question in the room:
wet, dripping and mingling with sweat.
It's hard to age a person from their genitals
alone, much less the way they yearn.
Somewhere in a darkroom, a man pulls
secrets out of another man. We men have long
held our motives for coming, this non-place
its organic edges, for meeting eyes as if through
an amoeba's membrane. The lamps are dimmed,
we all believe, to preserve fantasy; we fear light
will reveal how gently we touch ourselves.

SNOW

Tool-rough palms guide his brother's foamy hand.

Get that bit under your chin.

There over the bathroom sink

he sees a million lives in his brother's

eyes.

They're expressive now as his brother reaches out, trying to paint
his nose

white.

C'mon, don't be a silly bugger. He rinses the blade under the run-
ning tap

holds it gently to taut skin.

Stand still now.   One time, as he lay in bed

with a girl   she asked him his deepest secret. He

lied.

His brother has given up asking what it's like to go with someone.

He wishes he could have told him.

There are still so many things he wishes he could

understand.

He has never prayed for himself but every night

he prays for his brother to get better.

Still picks the skin around his nails, probably will

forever.

Mam'll have a fit if I nick you.

The razor moves as if peeling a film of air

from a pressed flower.

For the first time he sees his brother's face
glistening, wet. A fresh patch of earth.

To look at it, you would believe anything could grow there.

WHITE SOFT PARAFFIN

When at a young age your body's boundary / desiccates / when folded sheet of mudcracked skin / you learn many big words / pruritic / atopic / lichenification /

Mother / ceremonious with her emollients / milky baths / occlusives / little-fingerfuls of hydrocortisone / would put me to bed oily / as a marine mammal feels /

It's an undefined border / topical steroid addiction / Biology kindling bushfires / across your dark country / you boiling to death from the inside / the only release / gouging thinning tissue /red streaks on bed sheets / badlands /engulfing backs of knees /

When paring fingernails failed / mother taped my hands in cotton gloves /

Imagine yourself bound /stinging nettle dangled / just near enough / to your eyelid / that a low breeze lets it peck / now remember / your impuissant / hands /

I still loathe this body under moonlight / would give up my nation in an instant / for gratification

THE SLOW ERASURE OF THE AUTHOR

Your local pizzaiolo has begun to lay
roses in the fridge, little red envelopes,
plugging gaps your beers leave behind.
Drinkers can locate an ice cube in snow,
truffle out all the dark corners of homes.
Finishing school alumni, walking in
straight lines with plums in their mouths.
Every ███ you're always sparkling:
your husband's work barbecue, uncovered
blacked out in the sunroom, awarded
'Drunkest at Your Grandfather's Wake'.
Months you've ███ the quit ███
app, phone a loved one pocket-begging
to know how you're feeling right now.
Mood is ███ cascading █ —
the night always escaping on horseback.
For your last ███ to the
bar, ███ before dangling ███ you.
The audience, your husband, the pizzaiolo,
loves ███ so much, it brings them ███

On the far-off island of morning, a stranger
sits on sand, surrounded by boulders
he can't remember █████████████████

DREADFUL BODIES

The thick weave curtain,
dust's safe smell. He hears
nothing he shouldn't hear.
In the kitchen sink, fresh crabs
clack, he senses
their shells, the underwater tang,
doesn't think of the tinnies, lined up
empty on the kitchen top
or how crabs, faced with threat
self-amputate.
Then he begins to cut.

SNOWDREAMMOTHERFIGURE

i don't recall her name
      only how it belongs to the class
of women's names
      like Rita or Gaynor,
there to keep the playground safe

      the pitch markings,
black, yellow, blue,
      hidden with snow
she stands out in her rose-pink coat
      she is soft, the coat is big

      Rita or Gaynor unzips
the front of herself
      laughs as i slot
my small, strange body
      into the gap that opens

      like the inside of a cupboard,
my eyes were often rubbed red,
      this fact is hazy,
i never feel cold
      i remember how safety feels

FLIGHT FEATHERS

When I was younger, I wished
for my arms to dislocate,
for my bones to crack
and re-form at fresh angles, new joints.

        I wished for my skin
           to prickle
             and sprout
                 with a fuzzy down

that would eventually
fall out,

and return
as flight feathers
      to carry me
           away.

I. Eros

MERCY
after Mary Oliver

Had it lived
sooner or later, it would have died.
You see
I'd have carried it outstretched
wherever I went. Nights alone I dreamt
the sweet ways of its dying,
used to edge myself
to its last breath's border.
Stranger, I could still kiss your hands
for their mercy, how
you didn't break eye contact
not once, the whole time
you held its head underwater.

XI

The Interior of a Heart

AFTER the incident ⬛⬛⬛⬛, the intercourse ⬛⬛⬛ was ⬛⬛ of another ⬛⬛⬛ ⬛⬛ quiet depth ⬛ ⬛⬛ more intimate ⬛ than ⬛⬛ ever wreaked upon ⬛⬛⬛ himself ⬛ all ⬛⬛, the remorse, the agony, the ⬛⬛ repentance, ⬛⬛⬛, expelled ⬛ ⬛⬛ from the ⬛⬛ ⬛⬛ heart ⬛⬛ and forgiven, ⬛⬛ ⬛⬛ that dark treasure ⬛ lavished on the very man ⬛ ⬛⬛ so adequately ⬛⬛ ⬛⬛ shy and sensitive ⬛⬛ ⬛⬛ his victim ⬛ ⬛⬛, pardoning ⬛ ⬛⬛ his black devices. ⬛

118

GOD IN A BATHHOUSE

Take a look at a Michelangelo,
the one with God in a bath.
God letting the water out, or

putting the plug back in,
God in a bathhouse with hot bathmates.
We shared a room once.

Five years ago, I slept
in your bed with your husband,
kissed him first.

I didn't mean to stay, I promise
as if it would change anything.
All of life is tricking the head cop.

In the centre of the Atlantic,
news reports say men
are boarding lifeboats

before the women and children,
others are taking the propeller's
way out. It has nothing to do

with a starving idea
everything to do with plucking
a single red grape from a bunch

in a supermarket aisle. Language,
to Nietzsche, is a gaoler.
The poet is always pacing a cell.

In the film, she's doing the mambo
on a log, the lead holding her,
her pretending to fall, hips swaying

as she stumbles, he's weeping.
If you dropped both words
on the moon, they'd land together.

God the iceberg, God pacing
his moon-cell, God in a bathhouse lifted
from water.

FACEBOOK TELLS ME YOUR PARENTS' HOUSE IS FOR SALE

How old
    were we? You don't have to answer.
Space is never rendered faithfully in a dream,
    your bedroom now a guest room,
no more football bedspread, same window sucking
    in light. Who recalls which of us started the game?

Shame™ the board game
    kept in the closet, no rules on how old
you must be to play. Remembering is like sucking
    a soggy paper straw, cheeks aching for an answer.
Last time I saw you, in the crematorium,
    you didn't reply. I get it. I still have the dream,

where I'm cycling fast on a dark street. It's how I know you dream.
    Did it make you feel anything, our game?
Strange trophy? sweet mouthful of turf? sin bin?
    Do you remember me old-
er, wonder how it started? You don't have to answer.
    I spent years sucking

the same straw, sucking
    until my cheeks burned. Can I confess that in the dream
when I go over the handlebars, I wake up. The answer,
    the ground was a lie, the game just a game.
Maybe you've learned this now we're old,
    maybe you're still trapped in that toilet stall.

They make the most innocent pets, brine shrimp, tanks
    so hazy, you don't know what they're really doing
when they hold each other. Adults by one week old,
    under stress they put themselves in cryptobiosis. Do they dream
in the hidden life? Of games
    they played together, filtering an answer?

You're a poem, I know you can't answer.
    We're changed when put back in a room.
I'm sorry, I don't regret the game,
    sorry for sitting here in the corner sucking
in light, unafraid of the dream
    that something broke us when we were ten years old.

CONCRETE QUARTERLY

The straight boy in the high-rise flat kissed
like he was growing a pearl under his tongue;
to sleep beside him was to share a bed
with a brutalist building. The straight boy
was studying a degree for which his subscription
to *Concrete Quarterly* would likely come in handy,
and that would make his parents proud.
When we first fucked, I could tell at least once
he'd sunk a body part into wet cement, felt relief
from the blurred boundary. It was sexy at first,
the hewn, passable façade, his deep quarry of mouth.
How we love to fetishise things that cause us harm.
As he came, he recited the formula for concrete's
tensile strength so precisely, it betrayed a childhood
practicing in a mirror. I saw then, the straight boy:
Impossible Construction, uninhabitable, folding
back into himself. Found us lying in petrified sheets,
white dust on the places I let him put his hands.

TENDING

Eleonora Pucci snaps blue latex
over a wrist like a *badante*
readying her caregiving rite.

She scans his marble skin, attentive
to tiny fractures at ankles, counts webbed
fibres in sculpted locks of age-bleached hair.

Personal care is even more tender
than intercourse. I recall the clenched stitch,
tasked with washing a man older than my father,

expected gloved hands to waver,
ground beef strained in cheesecloth—
as he disrobed, I kept a towel between us

not, as I'd have thought, to guard my eyes
but in the way a mother bird furls her wing
around breakable young.

My hands bearing for the first time
his softened mass, were steadfast,
pure as bathwater.

Eleonora climbs a scaffold, taller
than three of her, to look into David's cordate
eyes, sets her gentle tools to task.

CLOTH MOTHER

At thirty years fresh I've cut my thumb
on a bread knife's hungry edge.
I was making brunch.

It's so familiar, my blood
marbling the porcelain sink. A gules crest.

On the opposing thumb I have a waning sickle—
a footnote to the glass bottle opened with a brick wall.
Three waiter's friends have since gathered
like devil's toenails in my kitchen drawer.

I can still smell the knife-sweet wine.

I am over one thousand miles from home, look
we keep washing machines in the bathroom here!
The Ripasso is complicated and rich!

Still I call you, as if limping
up the road with gushing knee, cloth mother.

Fretting it needs stitches
I hold my phone camera to the cut.
You prescribe two plasters instead.

My husband will later joke about
your wire tongue.
He can't hear the glottal softness of your plosives.

Doesn't see that I could peel the film from my own plaster
press it around myself.

You ask if they sell Sudocrem here.
I have a washing machine in my bathroom!
The pharmacies have their own foreign-
sounding antiseptic. Yet I keep a small, grey tub
with red letters in the vanity.

I lift the lid just to think of you.

FOLLOWING A MILD ELECTRIC SHOCK I THINK OF ENGLAND

I'm no scientist but I've pressed
a D cell's
            nub
to my tongue,

which is to say
I know electricity.

Maybe you're right
I am biased.
The BS1363 plug: opposite of
            foreign
slips right in

correct in your hand,
an unforeseen keepsake, well-balanced
table knife.

Sometimes, as its earth is sliding
home,
I keep my index nested
between its pins
                  to feel

            buzzless,

      safe as a
      doorknob.

KLEPTOMANIA

No sooner has the plane touched down
than my fingers go itching to my pickings.
My left pocket offers a dish of lard
from which raises rosemary's woody head,
pilfered the day in your mother's yard
you taught me to spread it over *crescentine*.
I dog-ear a page of your family
album, cast iron *tigelle* pans
pressed together on a lit stove top
opposite a tableful of sharing hands.
Then from my ear I pull a stave of language—
       A tavola si può far arte.
My blunt tongue springs a summer peach:
hollow and singing as a cathedral.

I hold each in turn to the cold sun,
ask them if they are mine to keep

CARCIOFI

The year your mother cedes the kitchen
she gives me a bag of artichokes.
Picking one out, she warns me
to take care with the spines.
Her knife is blunt but familiar, her hands tire
opening up its stubborn head.
I take over. Your mother was raised on chestnuts
and things made of chestnuts or things
made from the flour of milled chestnuts.
È più quello che sprechi che quello che mangi,
she says, teaching me to test
when you've snapped away enough bracts
to find the tender middle. The last leaf
is always most sincere: yields
while holding form.
Your mother can still
fill a table to exhaustion. Amore,
I know it's hard seeing her this way.
Quick, while it's hot, let's eat. *A tavola.*

MY HUSBAND IS BUILDING A FARADAY CAGE

in our basement. He's worried about coronal holes
googles The Carrington Event often, thinks 'the big
one' is but a matter of time. *Back then*, he begins
as I stroke his hair in bed, *hardly anything was electric,*
but nowadays, imagine! When he does sleep, I feel his
warm body twitch beside mine, know he's dreaming
of markets crashing. My husband is a smart, smart man;
I haven't thought to ask him why. He's bought reels
of copper and a power saw, carefully measured the walls,
made space enough for two camp beds to fit. I've no idea
what a Faraday cage does, what it would protect us from.
If you could only see in his eyes what he fears to lose.
In undisturbed dreams, I'm a lucky coin he keeps with him.

NÉ

I regard my old name
tenderly in my palm.
A skimming stone.
You gave me this,
father. Taught me
to comb the shingle.
The ideal drakestone
is flat, you said,
the weight of an apple.
This new, lemon-bright
name feels heavy
as the word 'faggot'
scrawled on a bike shed.
I run my index along
its outer edge, curved:
a question. Square up
to the shore, cast
my name into its swell.
Four times it skips,
gravity failing, the stone
both swallowed and
firm in my mouth.

CONCAVE DISCO BALL

Sempre caro mi fu quest'ermo colle.
— Leopardi

I know from your window
the hill is insurmountable.
Trust me there's an escalator.
More of us survived this go around.
You don't have to fear
the top shelf anymore,

walk the underwear aisle
like a tourist. Those guys
who escaped Alcatraz
didn't drown, they're living
in Acapulco. Look, the hill
is flanked by other hills—

Dear God, kid, claw the wadded
tissue from your throat.
Soon this minute will seem
a small fraction of your life;
the inside of your skull
won't be mirrored forever.

I promise you, please.
I've seen how this ends for us.

ACKNOWLEDGEMENTS

Versions of some poems within this book have appeared in *And Other Poems, I'll Show You Mine, Pulp Poets Press, berlin lit, Strix, fourteen poems,* and *Magma.* I'm incredibly grateful to the editors of these stellar publications for offering early opportunities to share my work. Other poems are published or forthcoming, having placed in the Ledbury and Brotherton poetry prizes.

'THE BOYS ARE KILLING THEIR SIMS ON THE FAMILY PC' is after Andrew McMillan's 'the men are weeping in the gym', while 'Mercy' is after Mary Oliver's 'Pilot Snake'.

'The Interior of a Heart' uses text from Nathaniel Hawthorne's 'The Scarlet Letter', and 'Concave Disco Ball' begins with a line from Giacomo Leopardi's 'L'infinito'.

Poetry is a team sport: thank you to all those who have spent time with drafts of these poems and offered feedback. I have greatly enjoyed reading yours in return. With love and thanks to my family too who have always believed in my writing, especially Riccardo, my husband and most cherished soundboard.

Finally, thank you to Aaron for his delicate and enabling editorship, as well as to Caroline Bird, John McCullough, Alberto Pellegatta, Anthony Anaxagorou, Jack Underwood and Ella Frears for all of the teaching, mentorship, and support you have offered me along the way.

LAY OUT YOUR UNREST